Where Are You G

MW01025457

"I'm going where
I can *see* the water."

2

"I'm going where
I can *feel* the sand."

3

"I'm going where
I can *hear* splashing."

4

"I'm going where
I can *taste* lemonade."

5

"I'm going where
I can *smell* hot dogs."

6

H-m-m-m. *See* the water . . .

7

8

feel the sand . . .

hear splashing . . .

10

taste lemonade . . .

smell hot dogs.

"Are you going
to the beach?"

12

"No, I'm going to . . .

13

Grandma's house!"

"Me too!"